CHRISTMAS CAROLS

© International Music Publications Limited
Southend Road, Woodford Green
Essex IG8 8HN, England

215-2-370

The First Nowell

Moderato

REFRAIN

No - well,____ No - well, No - well, No - well!

A⁷　D　Bm　F♯m　D　G　D　A

Born is the King____ of Is - ra - el!

G　Dmaj⁷　G　D　D⁶　A⁷　D　A⁷　D

2 They lookèd up and saw a Star,
  Shining in the East, beyond them far,
  And to the earth it gave great light,
  And so it continued both day and night.
  　　　　　　　Nowell, *etc.*

3 And by the light of that same Star,
  Three wise men came from country far;
  To seek for a King was their intent,
  To follow the Star wherever it went.
  　　　　　　　Nowell, *etc.*

4 This Star drew nigh to the North-west,
  O'er Bethlehem it took its rest,
  And there it did both stop and stay
  Right over the place where Jesus lay
  　　　　　　　Nowell, *etc.*

5 Then entered in these wise men three
  Full reverently upon their knee,
  And offered there in His Presence
  Their gold, and myrrh, and frankincense.
  　　　　　　　Nowell, *etc.*

6 Then let us all with one accord,
  Sing praises to the heavenly Lord,
  That hath made Heaven and earth of nought
  And with His Blood mankind hath bought.
  　　　　　　　Nowell, *etc.*

Good King Wenceslas

Moderato

2 " Hither, page, and stand by me,
　　If thou know'st it, telling—
　Yonder peasant, who is he?
　　Where, and what his dwelling?"
　" Sire, he lives a good league hence,
　　Underneath the mountain;
　Right against the forest fence,
　　By St. Agnes' fountain."

3 " Bring me flesh, and bring me wine,
　　Bring me pine-logs hither;
　Thou and I will see him dine,
　　When we bear them thither."
　Page and monarch forth they went,
　　Forth they went together,
　Through the rude wind's wild lament,
　　And the bitter weather.

4 " Sire, the night is darker now,
　　And the wind blows stronger;
　Fails my heart, I know not how,
　　I can go no longer."
　" Mark my footsteps, good my page
　　Tread thou in them boldly;
　Thou shalt find the winter's rage
　　Freeze thy blood less coldly."

5 In his master's steps he trod,
　　Where the snow lay dinted:
　Heat was in the very sod
　　Which the saint has printed.
　Therefore, Christian men, be sure—
　　Wealth or rank possessing—
　Ye who now will bless the poor,
　　Shall yourselves find blessing.

Silent Night

Slowly

1. Si - lent Night! Ho - ly Night! All is calm, all is bright.

Round yon Vir - gin Mo - ther and Child! Ho - ly In - fant so ten - der and mild

Sleep in hea - ven - ly peace, _____ Sleep _____ in hea - ven - ly peace. _____

2 Silent night! Holy night!
Shepherds quake at the sight!
Glories stream from Heaven afar,
Heav'nly host sing Alleluia,
Christ the Saviour, is born!
Christ the Saviour, is born!

3 Silent night! Holy night!
Son of God, love's pure light
Radiant beams from Thy holy face,
With the dawn of redeeming grace
Jesus, Lord, at Thy birth,
Jesus, Lord, at Thy birth.

God Rest You Merry, Gentlemen

2 In Bethlehem, in Jewry,
    This blessèd Babe was born,
And laid within a manger,
    Upon this blessèd morn;
The which His Mother Mary
    Did nothing take in scorn.

O tidings, *etc.*

3 From God our Heavenly Father,
    A blessèd Angel came;
And unto certain Shepherds
    Brought tidings of the same:
How that in Bethlehem was born,
    The Son of God by name.

O tidings, *etc.*

© 1986 International Music Publications, Woodford Green, Essex IG8 8HN

4 " Fear not then," said the Angel,
  " Let nothing you affright,
  This day is born a Saviour
  Of a pure Virgin bright,
  To free all those who trust in Him
  From Satan's power and might."
                                O tidings, *etc.*

5 The shepherds at those tidings,
  Rejoicèd much in mind,
  And left their flocks a-feeding,
  In tempest, storm, and wind :
  And went to Bethlehem straightway,
  The Son of God to find.
                                O tidings, *etc.*

6 And when they came to Bethlehem,
  Where our dear Saviour lay,
  They found Him in a manger,
  Where oxen feed on hay;
  His blessèd Mother Mary
  Unto the Lord did pray.
                                O tidings, *etc.*

7 Now to the Lord sing praises,
  All you within this place,
  And with true love and brotherhood,
  Each other now embrace;
  This holy tide of Christmas,
  All other doth efface.
                                O tidings, *etc.*

While Shepherds Watched

Moderato

2 " Fear not," said he; for mighty dread
  Had seized their troubled mind;
  " Glad tidings of great joy I bring
  To you and all mankind."

3 " To you in David's town this day
  Is born of David's line
  A Saviour, who is Christ the Lord;
  And this shall be the sign."

4 " The heavenly Babe you there shall find
  To human view display'd,
  All meanly wrapp'd in swathing bands,
  And in a manger laid."

5 Thus spake the seraph, and forthwith
  Appear'd a shining throng
  Of Angels praising God, who thus
  Address'd their joyful song.

6 " All glory be to God on high,
  And to the earth be peace,
  Good-will henceforth from Heav'n to men
  Begin and never cease."

See amid the Winter Snow

Moderato

1. See a-mid the win - ter snow, Born for us on earth be - low See, the Lamb of God ap-pears; Prom-is'd from e - ter - nal years Hail, thou e - ver bles - sed morn!

Hail, re-demp-tions hap-py dawn! Sing thro' all Je - ru - se-lem! Christ is born in Beth-le-hem.

2 Lo, within a manger lies
He who built the starry skies,
He who throned in height sublime
Sits amid the cherubin.
         Hail, etc.

3 Say, ye holy shepherds, say,
What your joyful news to-day,
Wherefore have ye left your sheep,
On the lonely mountain steep?
         Hail, etc.

4 As we watched at dead of night,
Lo, we saw a wond'rous light,
Angels, singing peace on earth,
Told us of our Saviour's birth.
         Hail, etc.

5 Sacred Infant, all divine,
What a tender love was thine,
Thus to come from highest bliss
Down to such a world as this.
         Hail, etc.

6 Teach, O teach us, Holy Child,
By thy face so meek and mild,
Teach us to resemble Thee,
In thy sweet humility.
         Hail, etc.

The Holly and the Ivy

2 The holly bears a blossom,
  As white as lily flower;
And Mary bore sweet Jesus Christ,
  To be our sweet Saviour.
    O the rising, *etc.*

3 The holly bears a berry,
  As red as any blood
And Mary bore sweet Jesus Christ,
  To do poor sinners good.
    O the rising, *etc.*

4 The holly bears a prickle
  As sharp as any thorn
And Mary bore sweet Jesus Christ,
  On Christmas day in th' morn.
    O the rising, *etc.*

5 The holly bears a bark,
  As bitter as any gall;
And Mary bore sweet Jesus Christ,
  For to redeem us all.
    O the rising, *etc.*

6 The holly and the ivy
  Now both are full well grown,
Of all the trees that are in the wood,
  The holly bears the crown.
    O the rising, *etc.*

Sleep, Holy Babe!

Slowly

1 Sleep, Holy Babe! upon Thy mother's breast; Great Lord of earth, and sea, and sky, How sweet it is to see Thee lie, In such a place of rest; In such a place of rest.

2 Sleep, Holy Babe! Thine Angels watch around,
All bending low with folded wings,
Before th' Incarnate King of kings,
In rev'rent awe profound,
In rev'rent awe profound.

3 Sleep, Holy Babe! while I with Mary gaze
In joy upon that Face awhile,
Upon the loving infant smile,
Which there divinely plays,
Which there divinely plays.

4 Sleep, Holy Babe! ah! take Thy brief repose;
Too quickly will Thy slumbers break,
And Thou to lengthen'd pains awake,
That Death alone shall close,
That Death alone shall close.

The Coventry Carol

2 O sisters too, how may we do,
   For to preserve this day,
   This poor Youngling for whom we sing,
   Bye, bye, lully, lullay.

3 Herod the King in his raging,
   Chargèd he hath this day
   His men of might, in his own sight,
   All children young to slay.

4 Then woe is me, poor child, for Thee,
   And ever mourn and say,
   For Thy parting nor say, nor sing,
   Bye, bye, lully, lullay.

O Come all ye Faithful

2 God of God,
   Light of light,
   Lo, He abhors not the Virgin's womb;
   Very God,
   Begotten, not created;
   O come, let us adore him, *etc.*

3 Sing, choirs of Angels,
   Sing in exultation;
   Sing, all ye citizens of Heaven above,
   " Glory to God
   In the highest "
   O come, let us adore him, *etc.*

4 Yea, Lord, we greet Thee,
   Born, this happy morning;
   Jesus, to Thee be glory given;
   Word of the Father
   Now in flesh appearing;
   O come, let us adore him, *etc.*

© 1986 International Music Publications, Woodford Green, Essex IG8 8HN

Once in Royal David's City

Moderato

Mary was that Mother mild, Jesus Christ her little child.

2 He came down to earth from Heaven
   Who is God and Lord of all,
And His shelter was a stable,
   And His cradle was a stall;
With the poor, and mean, and lowly,
Lived on earth our Saviour Holy.

3 And, through all His wondrous Childhood,
   He would honour and obey,
Love, and watch the lowly Maiden,
   In whose gentle arms He lay;
Christian children all must be
Mild, obedient, good as He.

4 For He is our childhood's pattern,
   Day by day like us He grew,
He was little, weak, and helpless,
   Tears and smiles like us He knew;
And He feeleth for our sadness,
And He shareth in our gladness.

5 And our eyes at last shall see Him,
   Through His own redeeming love,
For that Child so dear and gentle,
   Is our Lord in Heav'n above;
And He leads His children on
To the place where He is gone.

6 Not in that poor lowly stable,
   With the Oxen standing by
We shall see Him, but in Heaven,
   Set at God's right hand on high;
When like stars His children crown'd
All in white shall wait around.

Christians Awake

Brightly

1. Christians a - wake, sa - lute the hap-py morn, Where - on the Sa-viour of the world was born;

Rise to a - dore the mys-ter-y of love, Which hosts of An-gels chant-ed from a - bove;

With them the joy - ful tid-ings first be - gun Of God in - car-nate and the Vir - gin's Son.

2 Then to the watchful shepherds it was told,
Who heard th' angelic herald's voice, " Behold,
I bring good tidings of a Saviour's birth,
To you and all the nations of the earth;
This day hath God fulfill'd His promis'd word,
This day is born a Saviour, Christ the Lord."

3 He spake; and straightaway the celestial choir
In hymns of joy, unknown before, conspire;
The praises of redeeming love they sang,
And heaven's whole orb with Alleluias rang;
God's highest glory was their anthem still,
Peace upon earth, and unto men good-will.

4 To Bethl'hem straight th' enlighten'd shepherds ran,
To see the wonder God had wrought for man,
And found, with Joseph and the Blessed Maid,
Her Son, the Saviour, in a manger laid;
Then to their flocks, still praising God, return,
And their glad hearts with holy rapture burn.

5 O may we keep and ponder in our mind
God's wondrous love in saving lost mankind;
Trace we the Babe, who hath retrieved our loss,
From His poor manger to His bitter cross;
Tread in His steps, assisted by His grace,
Till man's first heav'nly state again takes place.

6 Then may we hope, th' angelic hosts among,
To sing, redeem'd, a glad triumphal song
He that was born upon this joyful day
Around us all His glory shall display;
Saved by His love, incessant we shall sing
Eternal praise to heav'n's almighty King.

Angels From the Realms of Glory

1. An-gels from the realms of glo - ry, Wing your flight o'er all the earth; Ye who sang cre-a - tion's sto - ry, Now pro-claim Mes - si - ah's birth. Glor - - - - - - - - - i - a, In ex - cel - sis De o, Glor - - - - - - - - - - i - a, In ex - cel - sis De - - o

2 Shepherds in the fields abiding,
    Watching o'er your flocks by night,
    God with man is now residing,
    Yonder shines the infant light;
            Gloria, *etc.*

3 Sages, leave your contemplations,
    Brighter visions beam afar;
    Seek the great Desire of nations,
    Ye have seen His natal star;
            Gloria, *etc.*

4 Saints before the altar bending,
    Watching long in hope and fear,
    Suddenly the Lord, descending,
    In His temple shall appear: Gloria, *etc.*

Away In A Manger

Slowly

2 The cattle are lowing,
  The Baby a-wakes,
But little Lord Jesus
  No crying He makes,
I love Thee, Lord Jesus!
  Look down from the sky,
And stay by my bedside
  Till morning is nigh.

3 Be near me, Lord Jesus,
  I ask Thee to stay
Close by me for ever,
  And love me, I pray;
Bless all the dear children
  In Thy tender care,
And bring us to heaven,
  To live with Thee there.

Good Christian Men, Rejoice

2 Good Christian men, rejoice
   With heart, and soul, and voice;
      Now ye hear of endless bliss:
         Joy! Joy!
   Jesus Christ was born for this:
   He hath oped the heavenly door,
   And man is blessèd evermore.
      Christ was born for this:
      Christ was born for this:

3 Good Christian men, rejoice
   With heart, and soul, and voice;
      Now ye need not fear the grave:
         Peace! Peace!
   Jesus Christ was born to save!
   Calls you one and calls you all,
   To gain His everlasting hall:
      Christ was born to save!
      Christ was born to save!

It came upon the midnight clear

Moderato

1. It came up-on the mid-night clear, that glor-ious song of old, From an-gels bend-ing

near the earth, To touch their harps of gold. "Peace on the earth, good-will to men, From

heav'n's all gra-cious King" The world in sol-emn still-ness lay, To hear the an-gels sing.

2 Still through the cloven skies they come,
  With peaceful wings unfurled,
And still their heavenly music floats
  O'er all the weary world;
Above its sad and lowly plains
  They bend on heavenly wing,
And ever o'er its Babel-sounds
  The blessèd angels sing.

3 Yet with the woes of sin and strife
  The world has suffered long;
Beneath the angel-strain have rolled
  Two thousand years of wrong;
And man, at war with man, hears not
  The love-song which they bring:
O hush your noise, ye men of strife,
  And hear the angels sing!

4 For lo! the days are hastening on,
  By prophet-bards foretold,
When with the ever-circling years
  Comes round the age of gold:
When peace shall over all the earth
  Its ancient splendours fling,
And the whole world send back the song
  Which now the angels sing.

© 1986 International Music Publications, Woodford Green, Essex IG8 8HN

What Child is this?

Moderato
F minor (Doh = Ab)

2 Why lies He in such mean estate,
  Where ox and ass are feeding?
  Good Christian, fear; for sinners here
  The silent word is pleading;
  Nails, spear, shall pierce Him through,
  The cross be borne, for me, for you;
  Hail, hail, the word made flesh,
  The Babe, the Son of Mary.

3 So bring Him incense, gold and myrrh,
  Come peasant, king, to own Him,
  The King of Kings salvation brings,
  Let loving hearts enthrone Him.
  Raise, raise the song on high,
  The Virgin sings her lullaby;
  Joy, joy, for Christ is born,
  The Babe, the Son of Mary.

Hark! The Herald Angels Sing

Moderato

2 Christ, by highest heav'n ador'd,
Christ, the everlasting Lord,
Late in time behold Him come,
Offspring of a Virgin's womb.
Veil'd in flesh the Godhead see!
Hail, th' Incarnate Deity!
Pleas'd as Man with man to dwell,
Jesus, our Emmanuel.
            Hark! the herald angels, *etc.*

3 Hail! the heav'n-born Prince of Peace!
Hail! the Sun of Righteousness!
Light and life to all He brings,
Ris'n with healing in His wings.
Mild He lays His glory by,
Born that man no more may die,
Born to raise the sons of earth,
Born to give them second birth.
            Hark! the herald angels, *etc.*

© 1986 International Music Publications, Woodford Green, Essex IG8 8HN

A Virgin Most Pure

2 In Bethlehem city, in Jewry it was,
Where Joseph and Mary together did pass,
And there to be taxed, with many one more,
For Caesar commanded the same should be so.
    Rejoice and be merry, etc.

3 But when they had entered the city so far,
The number of people so mighty was there,
That Joseph and Mary, whose substance was small,
Could get in the city no lodging at all.
    Rejoice and be merry, etc.

4 Then they were constrained in a stable to lie,
Where oxen and asses they usèd to tie;
Their lodging so simple, they held it no scorn,
But against the next morning our Saviour was born.
    Rejoice and be merry, etc.

5 The King of all Glory to the world being brought,
Small store of fine linen to wrap Him was bought;
When Mary had swaddled her young Son so sweet,
Within an ox-manger she laid him to sleep.
    Rejoice and be merry, etc.

6 Then God sent an Angel from heaven so high,
To certain poor Shepherds in fields where they lie,
And bid them no longer in sorrow to stay,
Because that our Saviour was born on this day.
    Rejoice and be merry, etc.

7 Then presently after, the Shepherds did spy,
A number of Angels appear in the sky,
Who joyfully talked, and sweetly did sing,
To God be all glory, our Heavenly King.
    Rejoice and be merry, etc.

We Three Kings of Orient Are

Still pro - ceed - ing, Guide us to Thy per fect light.

2 Born a King on Bethlehem plain,
Gold I bring to crown Him again
King for ever, ceasing never
Over us all to reign.

O star, etc.

3 Frankincense to offer have I,
Incense owns a Deity nigh:
Prayer and praising, all men raising,
Worship Him, God most high.

O star, etc.

4 Myrrh is mine, its bitter perfume
Breathes a life of gathering gloom;
Sorrowing, sighing, bleeding, dying,
Sealed in the stone-cold tomb.

O star, etc.

5 Glorious now, behold Him arise,
King, and God, and sacrifice!
Alleluia, Alleluia.
Earth to the heaven replies.

O star, etc.

I Saw Three Ships

Brightly

1. I saw three ships go sail - ing by, On Christ-mas Day,— on Christ-mas Day, I saw three ships go sail - ing by, On Christ-mas Day in the morn - ing

2 And what was in those ships all three
On Christmas Day, on Christmas Day.
And what was in those ships all three
On Christmas Day in the morning.

3 Our Saviour Christ and His lady,
On Christmas day, on Christmas Day.
Our Saviour Christ and His lady,
On Christmas Day in the morning.

4 And all the bells on earth did ring,
On Christmas Day, on Christmas Day.
And all the bells on earth did ring,
On Christmas Day in the morning.

The Seven Joys of Mary

Traditional English

be:_____ Praise Fa - ther, Son and Ho - ly Ghost To all e - ter - ni - ty.

G Am D   G C6 G   C   G D♯dim Em   Am   D   G

2. The next good joy that Mary had,
   It was the joy of two;
   To see her own Son Jesus Christ,
   Making the lame to go.
   Making the lame to go, Good Lord;
   And happy may we be;
   Praise Father, Son, and Holy Ghost
   To all eternity.

3. The next good joy that Mary had,
   It was the joy of three;
   To see her own Son Jesus Christ,
   Making the blind to see.
   Making the blind to see, Good Lord;
   And happy may we be;
   Praise Father, Son, and Holy Ghost
   To all eternity.

4. The next good joy that Mary had,
   It was the joy of four;
   To see her own Son Jesus Christ,
   Reading the Bible o'er.
   Reading the Bible o'er, Good Lord;
   And happy may we be;
   Praise Father, Son, and Holy Ghost
   To all eternity.

5. The next good joy that Mary had,
   It was the joy of five;
   To see her own Son Jesus Christ,
   Raising the dead to life.
   Raising the dead to life, Good Lord;
   And happy may we be;
   Praise Father, Son, and Holy Ghost
   To all eternity.

6. The next good joy that Mary had,
   It was the joy of six;
   To see her own Son Jesus Christ,
   Upon the Crucifix.
   Upon the Crucifix, Good Lord;
   And happy may we be;
   Praise Father, Son, and Holy Ghost
   To all eternity.

7. The next good joy that Mary had,
   It was the joy of seven;
   To see her own Son Jesus Christ
   Ascending into Heaven.
   Ascending into Heaven, Good Lord,
   And happy may we be;
   Praise Father, Son, and Holy Ghost
   To all eternity.

Wassail Song

19th Century Yorkshire

Allegro moderato

1. Here we come a - was - sail - ing A - mong the leaves so green,

Here we come a - wan - d'ring, So fair to be seen:

REFRAIN

Love and joy come to you, And to you your was - sail

too, And God bless you, and send___ you a hap - py new

F C7 F D7 Gm C7 F

D.C.

year, And God send you a hap - py new___ year.___

Gm C7 F D7 Gm C7 F Bb F

2. We are not daily beggars
   That go from door to door,
   But we are neighbours' children
   Whom you have seen before:

   Refrain

3. We have got a little purse
   Of stretching leather skin;
   We want a little money,
   To line it well within:

   Refrain

4. God bless the master of this house,
   Likewise the mistress too;
   And all the little children,
   That 'round the table go:

   Refrain

5. Good master and good mistress,
   While you're sitting by the fire,
   Pray think of us poor children
   Who wander in the mire:

   Refrain

Deck the Hall with Boughs of Holly

Old Welsh Carol

2. See the blazing Yule before us,
   Fa la la la la, la la la la,
   Strike the harp and join the chorus,
   Fa la la la la la, la la la la.
   Follow me in merry measure,
   Fa la la la la la la,
   While I tell of Yuletide treasure,
   Fa la la la la, la la la la.

3. Fast away the old year passes,
   Fa la la la la, la la la la,
   Hail the new, ye lads and lasses,
   Fa la la la la, la la la la.
   Sing we joyous all together ,
   Fa la la la la la la,
   Heedless of the wind and weather,
   Fa la la la la, la la la la.

Printed in Great Britain by Hobbs the Printers Ltd, Totton, Hampshire 2/98